MW01007379

The
Broken Branch
"An Orphan epidemic"

Yan Venter

DEDICATION

I dedicate this book to the many who work hard in these troubled times, to build a real home.

May the Lord grant you favor to go to the regions beyond and to discover the joy of fulfilling your destiny

FOREWORD

It has been my privilege to know Yan Venter for more than twenty five years.

We became friends shortly after Yan and his family moved to the States from South Africa in 1985 and came to our church to minister. His powerfully anointed ministry was a turning point for our church and for my personal ministry.

We have played together and prayed together. We've laughed and cried together, through great triumph and great tragedy. And, through all the years and all the experiences, I have found him to be a man of great generosity, integrity and passion for lost souls and for the Body of Christ.

Therefore, it is my great privilege and pleasure to recommend this powerful message to all who set their minds to digest these vital truths.

As I read this manuscript, I found myself in its paragraphs, and I had to honestly evaluate my own personality quirks and weaknesses and then bring them to the cross of Christ for his healing and redemption.

I believe each reader will likewise find yourself in these lessons, and will find the personal peace and healing you have long needed.

Read prayerfully and be blessed, enriched and strengthened by the power of the Holy Spirit through His anointed vessel.

Dr. Larry Pyle

CONTENTS

A NOTE TO WOMEN

As you read this book, you will notice that I only use the term, "sons" and not daughters. I am NOT ignoring your own plight for recognition in life, but when the bible speaks of "sons" in this context, it includes women! The bible is clear about this when it teaches, that "In Christ, there is neither male, nor female…"

When God made Adam AND **Eve**, he called THEM, "Adam."

The orphaned heart and the writings in this book, very definitely applies to women in the home also. Our society is filled with orphaned daughters!

INTRODUCTION

During one of my recent visits to South Africa, I invited a group of seventeen pastors to accompany me. THIS IS something I often do, as I feel that it allows these pastors to broaden their world-vision.

This Pastors Conference was electrified by the power of God and the people were all hungry for the Word. A spirit of revelation impregnated the atmosphere as the Holy Ghost directed me to teach on the subject of the "*Orphan Heart In The Church.*"

It was one of those kind of meetings, which draws the preacher into the lap of the Holy Spirit. Men and women were crying as the truth about our days broke upon them like a sunrise on a cloudy day.

As I turned around to observe the rest of my group sitting behind me in a row, I was shocked to see they were not receiving the importance of this revelation. It was evident that they regarded it as only another sermon and not an insight into what really is happening all around us.

The world is in a state of confusion, families are breaking apart at an alarming rate, and our churches are still preaching the same message from a hundred years ago, unable to deal with the "issues of life" in a real way.

Churches have gotten pulled into *the system*. Incapable of dealing with the real issues. Instead of turning orphans into sons, they've converted their churches into "foster homes." Hurting people are wondering in and out of these "institutions" without finding what they're looking for.

Christian homes are breaking apart at an alarming increase and the situation is getting worst by the day.

"Counseling sessions" are arranged for victims of this invisible crime in our churches and few of these sessions have any success.

The teaching in this book is vital for the end time generation, before the great and terrible day of the Lord comes, according to Malachi. [1]

---

[1] Mal 4:5

As you read this book, let me challenge you to first look at yourself, look at your family and yes, look at your church.

Ask the Lord to bring this message to you as a revelation that will revolutionize your life in every aspect.

While your eyes glance over the pages, ask the Lord to help you step out onto the balcony of Heaven so that you can have a wider vision of how He looks at our world today. And while you're doing this, ask God to let you know, if YOU'RE a son/daughter according to His measurement, because so many are pastoring churches, themselves wounded by the arrows of rejection.

Everywhere I teach this truth, it is evident that some get it while others prefer to dwell in the twilight zone at the bottom of the mountain where many dance around the golden calves of their own imagination.

We are a city set on a hill and we're supposed to be a beacon of hope for the hurting. Why don't you decide with me today; religion has no right to hang it's shackles of confusion and deceit around our ankles?

It's time to step away from the dark shadows of your past into the sunlight of His plans for your life.

Turn the page now and go with me on this journey into a world of "Sonship" and yes, of "Fatherhood."

1 OUR FATHERS

_____

Absent Fathers

JOHANNESBURG - It was after the second or third animal corpse was found that conservationists at the Pilanesberg game reserve in South Africa realized they had a major problem: Someone, or something, was systematically killing rhinos, and the chief suspects were elephants.

Elephants don't normally kill rhinoceroses. So when the attacks began in April of that year, the game rangers on the reserve, north of Johannesburg, were reluctant to believe what was happening.

But the evidence, although baffling, was unmistakable.

Some of the dead rhinos had gaping wounds, shaped like elephant tusks, in their backs. Others had suffered broken ribs and internal injuries that could have been inflicted only by a much larger animal.

There were upturned and trampled trees at the death scenes - always a telltale sign of elephants. And finally, the giveaway of many a murder mystery, there were footprints...elephant footprints.

By June, the serial elephant killer or killers had claimed four confirmed rhino victims and six suspected ones whose corpses were too badly decayed to establish positively the cause of death.

But Greg Stuart-Hill, the region's chief ecologist, said there are few doubts that the six also had fallen prey to the same killers. The reserve normally registers one rhino death, of natural causes, every two or three years.

Ten more died in just three months that spring, and five were wounded. For the park's management, it was a nightmare.

The only recorded instances of elephants killing rhinos occurred at waterholes, when mothers with young calves felt threatened. But these killings did not occur near waterholes, and inquiries quickly eliminated the park's only two mother elephants from the list of suspects.

An old warden, who reminded them of what happened several years before, finally brought the answer to light.

In the late 1970s Pilanesberg became a pioneer in the restocking of animals. Baby elephants that would have been marked for slaughter in other parks (as part of the annual cull to keep elephant populations manageable) were moved instead to Pilanesberg along with two adult females to care for them.

Mothers normally drive male elephants from the herd once they reach adulthood. Males start drifting away around age 15, eventually linking up with other groups of male elephants led by a patriarch.

But now that Pilanesberg's elephants are reaching adolescence, there are no adult males for them to follow. Thus, they have become juvenile delinquents deprived of adult supervision or role models.

"There are no adult bulls around to keep them in check," Stuart-Hill said. "So they're highly aggressive and are testing their strength on other animals."

Clive Walker, chairman of the Rhino and Elephant Foundation of Africa, believes the problem goes back to the childhood trauma suffered by these translocated elephants and to the lack of parental authority throughout their formative years. [2]

It became clear to the owners that *the absence of fathers* amongst these young elephants were the main reason for their delinquent actions!,

So, immediate arrangements were made for two mature bulls to be brought into the herd, and to the amazement of the local wardens, the problem was immediately solved.

---

[2] **Liz Sly** - *Chicago Tribune – October 1994*

Marauding in Central Park

In a terrific article, "Of Elephants and Men," in the 'Fatherhood Today," magazine, Dr. Wade Horn, writes a story very similar to that of the elephants, though it happened not in Africa, but in New York's Central Park. The story involved young men, not young elephants, but the details were eerily close. Groups of young men were caught on camera sexually harassing and robbing women and victimizing others in the park. Their herd mentality created a sort of frenzy that was both brazen and contagious. In broad daylight, they seemed to compete with each other, even laughing and mugging for the cameras as they assaulted and robbed passersby. It was not, in any sense of the term, the behavior of civilized men.

Appalled by these assaults, citizens demanded a stronger and more aggressive police presence. Dr. Horn asked a more probing question. "Where have all the fathers gone?" Simply increasing the presence of police everywhere a crime is possible might assuage some political pressure, but it does little to identify and solve the real social problem behind the brazen Central Park assaults. It was the very same problem that victimized rhinos in that park in Africa. The majority of the young men hanging around committing those crimes in Central Park grew up in homes without fathers present.

That is not an excuse. It is a social problem that has a direct correlation with their criminal behavior. They were not acting like men because their only experience of modeling the behaviors of men had been taught by their peers and not by their fathers. Those who did have fathers had absent fathers, clearly preoccupied with something other than being role models for their sons. Wherever those fathers were, they were not in Central Park.

Dr. Horn pointed out that simply replacing fathers with more police isn't a solution. No matter how many police are hired and trained, they will quickly be outnumbered if they assume the task of both investigating crime and preventing crime. They will quickly be outnumbered because presently in our culture, two out of every five young men are raised in fatherless homes, and that disparity is growing faster as traditional family systems break down throughout the Western world.

Real men protect the vulnerable, not assault them. Growing up having learned that most basic tenet of manhood is the job of fathers, not the police. Dr. Horn cited a quote from a young Daniel Patrick Moynihan written some forty years ago:

"From the wild Irish slums of the 19th Century Eastern Seaboard to the riot-torn suburbs of Los Angeles, there is one unmistakable lesson in American history: A community that allows a large number of young men to grow up in broken homes, dominated by women, never acquiring any stable relationship to male authority, never acquiring any rational expectations for the future – that community asks for and gets chaos."

When Prisons Replace Families

A Priest from New Hampshire, who had spent a number of years behind bars himself, reported the following:

"It's easy in the politically correct standards of today to dismiss 'AWOL' fathers as chauvinistic. But while we're arguing that point, our society's young men are being tossed away by the thousands into prison systems that swallow them up. Once in prison, this system is very hard to leave behind. The New Hampshire prison system just released a dismal report two weeks ago. Of 1,095 prisoners released in 2007, over 500 were back in prison by 2010. Clearly, the loss of freedom does not compensate for the loss of fathers in managing the behavior of young men.

There is very little that happens in the punishment model of prison life that teaches a better way to a young man who has broken the law. The proof of that is all around us, but – especially in an election year – getting anyone to take a good hard look inside a prison seems impossible. We live in a disposable culture, and when our youth are a problem, we simply do what we do best. We dispose of them, sometimes forever. Anyone who believes that punishment, and nothing but punishment, is an effective deterrent of criminal behavior in the young is left to explain why our grotesquely expensive prisons have a 50 percent recidivism rate."[3]

---

[3] Father Gordon J. MacRae has served nearly 19 years of a prison sentence of 33½ to 67 years. Convicted of sex offenses, he has steadfastly maintained his innocence, even rejecting plea bargains that would have freed him years ago.

Imprinting

Did you hear the story about the duck that fell in love with a tricycle? Believe it or not, the story was true! It seems that after birth, ducks will imprint on, or become attached to, the first moving object they see. In the case of the duck in the story, the first moving object was a red tricycle.

One instinctive behavior of the bird family that appears remarkable to humans is a process called *imprinting*. During a critical period, typically immediately or shortly after birth, a baby bird will become permanently attached to the first moving object it sees. In the case of the bald eagle, the critical age for imprinting is between the time it is first able to focus its eyes (around 9 days) and six weeks of age. If the bald eagle receives care or food from a source other than a bald eagle, it will imprint on, or become permanently, emotionally attached to, that source.

This often happens when well-meaning people encounter an orphaned or injured bald eagle. By handling or feeding the eagle, these well-intentioned persons condemn the baby eagle to a lifetime of confinement or sure death in the wild. A bald eagle that has imprinted on a human will "fall in love" with the person it assumes is responsible for its care. The bald eagle then behaves as though it is human and seeks the company of humans rather than other members of its own species. This leads to a dangerous situation when the bald eagle approaches unwary humans for food or company. This may result in serious injury for the human and possible death for the misunderstood eagle.

Another unfortunate consequence for the bald eagle that has imprinted on a human is that the bald eagle may never be attracted to members of its own species. If this happens, the eagle will never find a mate and raise young.

While "imprinting" surely plays an important role in animals, it has long been a proven fact, that the same applies to the human family.

We commonly refer to these imprints as *"bad habits"* when we notice anything contrary to what is *"normal."* It's truly amazing how the human mind can adapt or attach to anything we allow to leave an imprint.

Always sweet and sensitive, Paula's 4-year-old completely

stunned her mother when she lashed out one day by calling her the "B" word. It didn't take a psychology degree to realize where that out-of-the-blue vulgarity came from: The little girl had walked through the living room the week prior when movie dialogue included the same crudity.

Isolated cases? I don't believe so. Consider these:

One father explained how his 5-year-old began misusing the Lord's name after getting an earful from an "innocent" animated feature.

A woman described how a scene in a motion picture led her to start cutting herself and further escalated her deep depression.

Positive imprints from parents in the lives of their children are vitally important, but it must be done in an environment of trust and love.

The typical amount of time a working parent spends with his/her young children is about 30 minutes per day.

A typical father (in our time). will spend less than three minutes per day alone with a child who has reached his/her teenage years. On average, American youth watch 1,500 hours of television per year. They spend 900 hours per year in class at school and less than a hundred hours per year in one-on-one activity with a parent. They see 20,000 commercials per year.[4]

When our kids are exposed to these influences, without much supervision, and are generally not guided to interpret their circumstances and opportunities in light of biblical principles, it's no wonder they grow up to be just as involved in gambling, adultery, divorce, cohabitation, excessive drinking and other unbiblical behaviors as everyone else.

When we don't leave positive imprints in the lives of our children, it is dangerously possible for someone else to leave theirs.

We have evolved a society wherein we pretend things are normal, while it certainly is not. The family life has deteriorated to a point where it has almost reached total collapse.

The disappearance of fathers is now nearly the norm. Almost one in four American children lives in a household without their biological dads.

Society has become an immoral pit of slime and teaches that it

---

4 Norman Herr, Ph.D., The Sourcebook for Teaching Science: Strategies, Activities, and Internet Resources, 2001, "Television & Health"

is okay for a man to be feckless.   It is acceptable for him to wander away because he is immature, selfish and young; for her to have a baby on her own because the clock is ticking and really, she doesn't need a man for anything more than sperm.

This is the new morality, the new American mindset.

We've become a confused society, and it's permeated throughout.   It's in our homes, it's on the street, it's in our government and now it's taking over our churches.

Recently President Barack Obama unveiled a new initiative, created through executive order and partnering with businesses and foundations to spend $200m over five years, *"to help young men of color stay out of prison, stay out of jail"*.

What an aspiration!

"This is an issue of national importance, "Obama said of his "My Brother's Keeper" program, aimed at black and Hispanic men. "It's as important as any issue that I work on."

Sadly, the message to the people is that we can't be expected to take individual responsibility for our lives, so the government has to do it for us.

But, parenting is the real problem here, not the often repeated media narrative of "The Troubled Black Teenager", upon which society inflicts so many ills.   On the contrary, it is the long overlooked and systemic problem of the broken black family.

The president knows the grim facts. "If you're African American, there's about a one in two chance you grow up without a father in your house – one in two," he said in his announcement. "We know that boys who grow up without a father are more likely to be poor, more likely to underperform in school." He went on:

"As a black student, you are far less likely than a white student to be able to read proficiently by the time you are in fourth grade. By the time you reach high school, you're far more likely to have been suspended or expelled. There's a higher chance you end up in the criminal justice system, and a far higher chance that you are the victim of a violent crime. And all of this translates into higher unemployment rates and poverty rates as adults."

What Obama conveniently left out of his narrow narrative is the root cause of the problems facing not just young black men but the American black family today: 72% of all black babies are born out of wedlock. Think about that: it's an *anomaly* for black children to be born to parents who are married. And that's where the overwhelming crime and economic malaise begins, among the 13% of the US population that is black.

Worse still, there is a direct correlation between kids born out of wedlock and higher rates of crime.[5]

While this quote from Crystal Wright, a black reporter from the Guardian, referenced the black community, it is also an accurate assumption of our entire society. We're falling apart, and we overlook the real problem, namely the family structure.

The solution does not lie with the Government or any kind of legislation, but in the fundamental principal of returning to the spiritual welfare of our homes.

During the Great Depression, unemployment, lower wages, and the demands of needy relatives tore at the fabric of family life. Desertions soared, and by 1940, 1.5 million married couples were living apart. Many families coped by returning to a cooperative family economy. Many children had to take part time jobs and many wives supplemented the family income by taking in sewing or laundry, setting up parlor groceries, or housing lodgers.

World War II also subjected families to severe strain. During the war, families faced a severe shortage of housing, a lack of schools and child-care facilities, and prolonged separation from loved ones. Five million "war widows" ran their homes and cared for children alone, while millions of older, married women went to work in war industries. The stresses of wartime contributed to an upsurge in the divorce fate. Tens of thousands of young people became latchkey children, and rates of juvenile delinquency, unwed pregnancy, and truancy all rose.

The "*Orphan Epidemic*" started and is rising to a level so dangerous that, just like the "delinquent elephant story" in the beginning of this chapter, our young men and women, our children and parents alike, are destroying everything in their paths.

---

[5] Crystal Wright from The Guardian. (Monday, 3 March 2014)

2 IT'S A WAR

America is engaged in a civil war. The battle lines are drawn, the strategies are in place, the casualties are mounting and the winner takes all.

From the shattering of families to a staggering rate of crime and lawlessness, the secular assault on the moral fabric of this country is unraveling every facet of life as we have known it. Even our most basic liberties, including our freedom to worship God without government interference and censorship, are now threatened.

It almost seems redundant to consider once again the statistics that, by now, have become familiar to most of us. On every side, in almost every place, we are beset with child abuse, rape, abortion that occurs at the rate of one per minute, drug abuse, senseless violence, sexual perversion, pornography, divorce, gang warfare, and finally, teenagers who are committing suicide at the rate of one every 90 minutes. No wonder.

It is not so much a situation in which Americans are merely breaking the law; it is more grave than that. It is a situation where people have actually overturned the law. God issued a severe warning to Israel in Isaiah 5:20: "Woe unto them that call evil good, and good evil; that put darkness for light, and light for darkness; that put bitter for sweet, and sweet for bitter!"

Boards of education across America sanction the teaching of homosexuality as an acceptable lifestyle, but the Supreme Court has banned them from using any reference to the word "God" in their official writings. We seem to have lost the standard, and there is no longer any consensus of what is true and what is honorable.

Ten years ago, we were shocked at revelations of declining moral values in America. Today, the shocking thing is that nothing shocks us anymore. We have seen it and heard it so many times that we have almost become desensitized. But as Christians accountable to God, we must wrestle with serious questions: How did this happen to our once great nation? What do we do and where do we go from here?

One thing is for sure; we cannot ignore the problem any longer. We must reclaim our land, but it must start in our homes.

Paul made it clear when he said, "That which is natural comes first."[6]

I hear churches pray for revival all throughout the land, and God knows we need it, but before this can be done, the family structure must be made right. As you read this book, ask the Lord to open your heart's understanding with all His might.

---

[6] 1 Cor. 15:46

Facing Reality

For those of us engaged in the study of end-time prophecies, there is a subtle danger in all of this. We read 2 Timothy 3:1-5, and we know that, in the latter days, men are destined to become selfish, proud, disobedient to parents, without natural affection, despisers of those that are good, and lovers of pleasure more than lovers of God.

We debate the conspicuous absence of the United States in the final biblical scenario, and we somehow conclude that maybe America's decay is just a predestined prelude to the return of our Savior, and so we have become passive in our approach.

But if our Lord did return today, what would we have left to give Him from the wreckage of our rich spiritual heritage and the incredible blessings that He has bestowed on this country? We know from the parable of the talents that God expects a return on the truth that He has invested in us. How many talents would we have to offer?

Whatever God chooses to do with the United States, we as Christians are still responsible for our stewardship of the liberties and the freedoms that He has given us. Jesus will not return in order to rescue us from a corrupt situation. He will return when His work on earth, through His church, is completed. The hope of His imminent return should compel us all the more to strive toward restoring the character of our country and the honor of His name.

It's plausible that the cause of our moral and spiritual dilemma, and the solution to it, may be something more simple and more profound than we have considered. Throughout Scripture, there seems to be a plan, ordered by God, that is designed to keep us corporately in God's blessing. It isn't just the type of government we set up or the people we elect or even the laws we institute. It is the simple commandment that we teach our children to keep the way of the Lord.

The concept goes back as far as Genesis 18:19 when God said of Abraham, *"For I know him, that he will command his children and his household after him, and they shall keep the way of the Lord, to do justice and judgment. . . ."* In Deuteronomy 4: 10, He states again *". . . and I will make them hear my words, that they may learn to fear me all the days that they shall live upon the earth, and that they may teach their children."*

The powerful impact of teaching children should not surprise us. Our enemies have understood it well. Communist countries made it policy to remove children from their homes at an early age in order to educate and indoctrinate them. Adolf Hitler pronounced that *"who controls the youth, controls the future."*

Liberal engineers of social change have made the claim that, given just one generation, they can radically alter a society. And they have proven their point.

Psalm 78:5-7 states: "For he established a testimony in Jacob, and pointed a law in Israel, which he commanded our fathers, that they should make them known to their children: That the generation to come might know them, even the children which should be born who should arise and declare them to their children: That they might set their hope in God, and not forget the works of God, but keep his commandments."

Perhaps we need to consider that God doesn't hold us as accountable for governments and policies and social orders as much as He does for the spiritual inheritance that we give to our own children. Perhaps, in His providential plan, it would be enough if only we would master the task of safeguarding God's truth from father to child, one generation at a time.

For many Christians, teaching our children God's truth may seem routine. But therein lies the danger. It doesn't mean that we passively sit back and tell our children what we believe. It doesn't mean that if they see us going to church and to Bible studies that they will somehow get the message.

Teaching is not just exhibiting faith but laboring to implant or imprint everything we know and understand about our God into the hearts and minds of the next generation. It is teaching God's Word and using every possible opportunity to demonstrate its validity. It is a labor of love.

Of His Word, God says: "And ye shall teach them to your children, speaking of them when thou sittest in thine house, and when thou walkest by the way, when thou liest down, and when thou risest up.... That your days may be multiplied, and the days of your children, in the land which the Lord swore unto your fathers to give them. . ." (Deut. 11:19-21).

Where Did America Get Off Track?

The fallout from the takeover of secular humanism in America has been staggering, and nowhere is it more evident than in the lives of our youth. When we examine the course of the last couple of decades in this country, we see a chronicle of what happens to a nation that turns its back on God.

The first chapter of Romans details a progression of sin and rebellion against God that is stunningly like the progression of life in America. It begins: "Because that, when they knew God, they glorified him not as God, neither were thankful; but became vain in their imaginations, and their foolish heart was darkened" (Rom. 1:21).

There is no lack of historical evidence that this country was founded on Christian principles. Document after document confirms an original commitment to God and to His laws.

Patrick Henry stated, "It cannot be emphasized too strongly or too often that this great nation was founded not by religionists but by Christians, not on religions but on the gospel of Jesus Christ."

After the Great Depression and the powerful impact of World War 11, a generation of Americans suddenly found themselves in a time of peace and prosperity. Life was easier, families were stable, and there was a general sense of order and rule.

Instead of obeying God's command to teach our children diligently, we delegated that responsibility to Sunday school teachers, public schools, and to authorities outside the home. At that time, there was no reason to assume that anything would be lost in the process. But we didn't see that the foundation was beginning to crumble.

Relationships were replaced by everything else and the mad chase after vanity left us with this generation of sinking vessels.

Give Kids a Benchmark

While the hearts of the children were at risk on the home front, their minds were being attacked on a different front. "And even as they did not like to retain God in their knowledge, God gave them over to a reprobate mind. . ." (Rom. 1:28).

Behavioral psychologists and secular forces began to infiltrate the public education system. Their influence gradually extended beyond academics and into the moral and philosophical realm.

Along with evolution, secularists brought with them the philosophy of humanism as set forth in two humanist manifestos, signed in 1933 and 1973. They introduced naturalism and supported it through the teaching of evolution. They replaced moral absolutes with relative values and situational ethics. And in 1962 they succeeded in persuading the Supreme Court to outlaw prayer and later, Bible reading, in the classroom. Quite an agenda for change.

Since that pivotal Supreme Court decision, teenage pregnancies have risen 556 percent and venereal disease is up 226 percent. Divorce, which had declined for 15 years, has tripled every year since, and S.A.T. scores, which had previously been stable, began their remarkable decline, which continues today.

It stands to reason, however, that the real problem came not because of what children were being taught in school. The real problem may have been what they weren't being taught at home.

How to Change the World

It appears that as a nation we have traveled the full spectrum from the loss of our Christian foundation to open rebellion against God's moral truth, which had led many into the realm of cultic beliefs and practices.

How do we begin to turn an entire nation around and to reclaim the godly heritage that once was ours? We begin one person at a time.

One of the enigmas of Christianity is that ever since Jesus chose a handful of men to change the course of history, God has carried on His master plan for the ages through the transformation of one life at a time. We are not asked to perform supernatural feats or to overthrow principalities. We change America the same way we change our families. Lives are turned around, when one on one, we are willing to be used by God to make known the gospel of Jesus Christ.

Someone once said that the darkest place of any lighthouse is always at its base. The same can be said of our families. A pastor or Christian leader can shine a radiant beam out to the horizons, warning passing ships of dangerous waters, while their own unmaintained plumbing floods the home.

At the core of who I am as a leader is the health and closeness of my family. And so it is for you, my friend. Fight for it. Fight as fiercely as Nehemiah urged his countrymen to fight when the enemies of God and Israel sought to destroy the work of rebuilding the nation (see Neh. 4:14).

If you miss building that home base, you will have nowhere to go when your ministry days are over. You'll arrive back on your doorstep with your boxes of books and notes, and you'll have nothing to walk into—except shards of yesterday's mistake of putting your job, ministry or career ahead of everything else. Restore the pre-eminence of the family early on. Too many have sacrificed marital harmony and family on the altar of success. It's not worth it.

Here's a fact—not a judgment, mind you. Just a fact of life. Although everyone in our great church loves the Venter family, I have come to realize that nobody is fighting for my family. That's my job, the task God has given to me. Others may fight for my time and energy, but no one will fight for my family.

My greatest ministry will be in the next generation. There came a point in David's life when he started storing gold and building materials so that his boy, Solomon, would have a free hand in building the Lord's temple. He had to switch his thinking when his life crossed the halfway point. He had to coach more and do less. His greatest contribution would be leading others to their greatest potential rather than accomplishing more personally. Of course he would still achieve much more, but he would soon come to grips with his humanity.

Now as a grandparent, I'm finding that truth coming to bear on my life in ever-increasing ways. My responsibility doesn't end where my empty nest begins. It continues. It must carry on into the generation of my grandchildren. I am not done yet!

3 ORPHANED FATHERS

The problem with a "sick" plant, most often lies in the roots. What you see above ground in your plants is really determined by what you can't see that's underground? What happens underground, where the plant roots live, drives plant growth. The bigger and healthier the root system, the bigger and healthier the plant.

> "The orphan spirit cannot be cast out; it can only be displaced by love."
> Jack Frost

The problem with our generation today, really stems from the fatherhood or absence thereof in our society, which is the very root of our existence.

Our children becomes a product of who we are and before the situation with our children can be fixed, our own problems need to be addressed first.

The problem is that we fail to recognize it. We become so cognizant of the children's problems but fail to turn to the roots. The children are merely the branches that will someday bear the fruit. Right now, it is time to ask God to reveal the condition of the roots in _your_ life.

In our society, we are dealing with "_broken branches,_" separated from the tree of life, resulting in orphaned attitudes. This problem does not lie only with our children, but parents themselves, as broken branches from their parental tree.

This is where we have to rely on the Holy Ghost to reveal our own shortcomings. It will demand a visit to your own past and where it started with _you_.

As I go around teaching these principles, it is obvious to me that fathers are walking around with blindfolds, unable to recognize their own problems in this matter.

In Mathew 13, Jesus was asked by the disciples, why He spoke to them in parables, and he answered, *"Therefore, I speak to them in parables, because seeing, they do not see, and hearing, they do not hear, nor do they understand."* Then he goes on to quote Isaiah:

"And in them the prophecy of Isaiah is fulfilled, which says, hearing you will hear, and shall not understand, and seeing you will see, and not perceive, for the hearts of this people have grown dull. Their ears are hard of hearing, and their eyes they have closed, lest they should see with their eyes, and hear with their ears, lest they should understand with their hearts and turn, so that I should heal them."

The same truth also applies to the church. (We'll address that later in this book) Pastors seem totally disconnected from the fact that they may have everything going, but there are no spiritual fathers.

We're not talking about men with gray hair. We're talking about men who have successfully generated spiritual sons with the imprint of "fatherhood" and "sonship" securely placed in them.

In the Spirit Realm

In the spirit realm, we have two kinds of fathers:

First, THE FATHER OF LIES. Satan generates orphans, because that is his nature. Because of his rejection and abandonment, he literally became the father of all spiritual orphans.

Second, THE FATHER OF LIGHTS. He generates sons.

Jesus made His mission clear when He promised his disciples (and us), *"I will not leave you as Orphans."*[7]

It is not only the things that happen in the natural world (our parents) that transform us into having "Orphan Attitudes," but the work of satan from the garden of Eden, continues his work still today.

Oft times, people are unable to recognize the "Orphan Spirit" in their own lives, or in those around us. Here's a few signs (Symptoms) to look for:

1. You feel parent-less with an inability to relate to the father of family.
2. You have the spirit of a loner. You are a person who prefers to be alone.
3. You have an inability to bond with people.
4. You suffer from loneliness and even feel alone even in the midst of family and friends.
5. You seem to be incapable of trusting people.
6. You have a rejection complex. It is easy for you to feel rejected or unwanted.
7. You struggle with knowing your identity.
8. You have a fear of intimacy and seem incapable of surrendering your inner life.
9. You experience unexplainable surges of anger at life.
10. You have a wandering spirit and feel like no place is home.
11. You are constantly feeling unloved and misunderstood.
12. You are insecure and unsure of everyone's true feelings.

---

[7] John 14:18.

The title of this book, *"The Broken Branch,"* refers to the orphaned heart.

Once the branch is broken off, it no longer draws from the nourishment of the root system and then withers away.

It can no longer bear any fruit, nor will it have the appearance of life.

Ever since Adam and Eve were alienated from God the Father in the Garden of Eden, an orphan spirit has permeated the earth, causing untold damage! (By "orphan," I am referring to a sense of abandonment, loneliness, alienation and isolation.) Almost immediately after the fall in Eden, the fruit of this orphan spirit resulted in jealousy, culminating in Cain murdering his brother Abel because God the Father didn't receive Cain's offering. To make matters worse, in contemporary society, with the breakup of the nuclear family, large amounts of people are not only alienated from God but are brought up without the loving care and security of their biological fathers.

I believe all of the emotional, physical and spiritual ills of society can be traced to humans feeling alienated from God *and their biological fathers.*

Orphaned men have a hard time connecting to their spouses, their children, those in spiritual authority and their supervisors. Additionally, they have a hard time accepting and loving themselves.

There are presently millions of incarcerated men who are acting out lives of violence and rebellion because their earthly fathers abandoned them. There are churches filled with pastors and leaders who use people and destroy relationships because they are driven to succeed. This is due to their need for a father's affirmation, which is a hole too large for ministry success or performance to fill.

The only way to break this orphan spirit is for people to be filled with a sense of the Father's love for them in Christ, which then enables them to become mature sons who serve God out of knowledge of His undeserved grace instead of trying to earn the Father's love through performance.

The orphan spirit is perhaps the greatest curse on the earth today. It will take spiritual parents with great spiritual depth and authority to break and reverse this curse to perpetuate a generational blessing. Only when a person is healed of fatherlessness through the love of God, is the orphan spirit broken so they can begin the process of entering mature sonship.

Sonship is so important that all creation is presently crying out for the manifestation of the mature sons of God![8]

Developing an Orphaned Heart ,follows a progression. In his book, "The Father's Embrace," Jack Frost lays it out best:

Twelve step progression to an Orphan Heart:

1. As a small child we **focus upon the faults** we see in parental authority. Hurt people hurt people. Parents are also hurting and then they hurt their children.
2. We receive their faults as disappointment, discouragement, grief, rejection, woundedness. How can you be a father if you were never a son, but a slave in your home? You treat your children as slaves as well.
3. Lose basic trust in parental authority. For example: I step accidentally on your foot – ask forgiveness – you still trust me as a person with integrity, etc. Next time I come by, you withdraw your foot. You trust me as a person BUT you've lost basic trust and won't let me come too close, you will withdraw. Life is a life of pain and rejection. We lose basic trust in relationships. We have relationships but we've lost basic trust. You lose it by the time you are 5 years old. If anyone gets too close, you move behind your walls of protection. Don't trust, don't talk, don't feel. I don't trust you enough to allow you to get near my feelings.

4. When you **lose** basic trust you move into a fear of submission in receiving love, comfort and admonishing from others. "I'll just do it myself."
5. Closed spirit – you close your heart to others.
6. You take on and Independent self-reliant attitude. "I'll just do it myself – I cant rely on anyone to do it for me." Independence, self reliance. You take care of everything, yourself included, so you can't cast your cares upon Jesus

---

[8] Rom 8:19

either.

7. We start **controlling** all our relationships
   - Independence and isolation
   - A fear of being hurt.
   - A fear of being known.
8. Our relationships then become superficial. We keep people at a distance.
9. Next, a stronghold is formed:
   - "No-one will be there for me."
   - Spiritual orphan-hood is formed.
   - Independent, self-reliant, rebellious attitude.
10. You begin your life as a spiritual orphan. You don't have a safe place. You will have to fight for everything, wrangle, argue.
11. Counterfeit affections:
    Passions of the flesh – You've got to bond to something. You were created for love, so you will bond to something.
    - Addictions – drug/food
    - Alcohol
    - Porn

    Possessions – worldly gain
    Position
    - Totally reliant of the praise of man.
    - Striving to be seen
    - Slaving away to be noticed.

    Power and control of your own life and destiny. Refuse to be real **or** open to admit your needs. Do not need anyone or anything. It only results in someone hurting you again, disappointing you, some always letting you down.

12. A life of oppression
    Heaviness, darkness, great difficulty, cannot receive any love and admonition from God and others. An independent spirit prevents you from acknowledging any needs or dependence.

We all know what an orphan is – a child with no parents. This is not the child's fault, and it is very sad when it happens. Even sadder is that often these children grow up deprived of key relationships and develop differently as adults, seeing the world in a different way.

Sometimes people grow up with parents of varying abilities and care, and yet are orphans (in their hearts) towards others, and especially toward leadership. We call this the orphan heart, and others have called it the orphan spirit. It's not the kind of spirit you can cast out because its actually the person themselves and the way they think and see themselves and the world around them.

Such a person is disconnected from others, finds it hard to trust people, especially leaders and often struggles with feeling inadequate, has low self-esteem and may feel resentment and other similar feelings. It is very hard for them to relax around spiritual leaders and to "give the heart" because their feelings don't let them. So, they develop the syndrome of "an orphaned heart."

Apostle Chuck Clayton used to tell the story of when, in his younger years in the ministry, he had a large church full of fine people who would do anything he asked of them. They were prepared to work hard. They would clean buildings and keep the grounds. They would participate in meetings and work at all aspects of the ministry. But Chuck could not understand why he felt he could never really trust them. He had puzzled for years why this was so, but later came to realize why. They had never given him their hearts!

Without the giving of our hearts to each other, trust is not established and intimacy cannot grow.

Without the giving of the heart there is no sonship. Without the giving of the heart, we have not laid aside our own agendas. Without the giving of the heart there is always room for an Absalom to arise, who deceives people, or steals away the ministry. You cannot build a work for God, you cannot build community, without the giving of the heart to each other in love, acceptance, and honor.

You may have sung a popular worship song in church with these words: "Come, now is the time to worship, now is the time to give our hearts."

Most people think that we must give our hearts to Christ and then we are born again. Yet, the message of sonship, and the whole new wineskin God is building, goes further. We must give our hearts to each other. Jesus said, "A new command I give to you, love one another." (John 13:34)

This is the giving of the heart, and it is all about fellowship with each other, as well as fellowship with God.

For people who struggle with fear of intimacy, self-esteem issues, and other feelings of rejection, there needs to be an acknowledgement of these issues, so that they can begin to be addressed. In church we have a number of stories of people who have miraculously overcome the orphan heart. These victories are possible when there is recognition, prayer, and willingness to work at something. The orphan heart <u>can</u> be conquered.

Our relationships are superficial because of a loss of basic trust. Loss of basic trust in family structures, in relationship, in church. Basic trust is the capacity to hold your heart out to another person.

You avoid people. Basic trust is not an issue between you and other people but it's between you and God.

For relationships to work they must be built on trust and initial respect. If I can't respect you there will be animosity in our relationship. If I can't trust you, there can't be a flow of relationship. Really, if I can't trust then, I cannot love!

If we want to have Godly relationships we must never break relationships on a negative note. A blow up in relationships is a way to control things. Agree with your adversity. Enter into Father's rest…a place of meekness and gentleness.

Relationships blow up when I focus on what man thinks of me. When I enter God's rest and know what God thinks of me, that is basic trust. I live life like I have a home, and I am secure. I do not need to take on the same spirit as the person that is attacking me. If I am subject to the Father, I am loved. Then God's grace comes in whatever the circumstances.

Basic trust: even when it hurts, you risk becoming vulnerable and keep your heart open. If you are secure in the Father's love you can move beyond the weaknesses in others and you can release God's love in the situation. You move back into the Father's love in every situation, even if they come at you in full anger. Even if someone is misrepresenting the Father's love to you, you can still be secure.

Look at this table:

SONSHIP	ORPHAN HEART
The Comforter	Accuser of the brethren
Innocence	My gift and position
Gentleness	Let people see me
Meekness	Cannot submit to anyone
Openness	Take everything as personal
Humility	Criticizing, judging
Liberty	Track record of broken heart
Rest	Escaping humanity
Health	Fight for everything
Wholeness	Manipulate and control
Mercy	Wrangle, trying to steal inheritance
Forgiveness	Undermining and judgmental
Not just physical healing, filled with joy and real happiness.	Making others look bad so you can look good. Sucking up to people to get things and position. Never satisfied, Always wants more.

Figure 1

3 BIBLICAL PRINCIPLES

It is very important that this question be well established with answerable facts in your life. Before you can become a father of any good quality, you have to be a son. There's absolutely no getting around this fact!

When you're a son, approved by the *Father of Lights*, you will produce "sons," who will carry the fruits from *your* life.

Remember the plant analogy earlier on in the book? It is simple to understand; "A peach tree will produce another peach tree – not something else. A banana plant will produce another one of it's kind and so on. Nothing will change this fact.

An orphaned father will produce orphaned sons and a father, well adjusted to the embrace of a father, will produce Godly sons!

Jesus made it clear that He would not leave His followers like orphans, but he made it clear, He was going to *"The Father's House,"* to prepare for them a mansion. Even when they asked Him to teach them how to pray, He showed them how to speak to the *Father*, praying; *"Our Father*, who art in heaven…"

Paul also made it clear when he said, "God did not give us the *spirit of bondage*, again to fear, you have received *the spirit of adoption*, whereby we cry, *Abba Father.*"[9]

The "spirit of bondage," is in fact, the "Orphaned Spirit!" The orphan does not have the luxury of:

- A Home. (Love)
- A Father. (Protection)
- Inheritance. (Security)
- Discipline. (Proper Development.)

People with an orphaned spirit live in continued bondage. Their bondage is under feelings of guilt, shame and an unfulfilled life. They also keep everyone else around them under bondage.

God wants you to enjoy the spirit of "sonship."

---

[9] Rom 8:15

God's Blueprint

It is VERY important that you take note of the fact; it is not everyone who qualifies to be "*a son.*"

When we come to Christ, we are a "*child of God,*" according to Paul,[10] but not yet a *son.* From the moment we accept Christ into our lives, we become born again. We are born into the family of God and we become a *child* of God. In the Greek, this denotes infantship.

He is very clear that *those* (only those) who are <u>led</u> by the Spirit, are sons.

Very little is recorded about the boy Jesus, in the Bible. We read about him when He was twelve years old, and then next, when He makes His appearance at the Jordan, to be baptized by John the Baptist.

It is at this very moment that we read how God spoke out of Heaven, saying, "This is My Beloved Son, in whom I'm well pleased.

From that very moment, His ministry started!

Paul mentions this "Sonship" of Christ, when He writes to the Hebrews, "*So Christ also glorified not himself to be made a high priest, but he that spake unto him, Thou art my Son, This day have I begotten thee.*"[11]

One cannot help but wonder, "**How** did we get it so wrong in the church?"

The same way Elisha's ministry started at the departure of Elijah when God raptured him into heaven. Till that moment, Elisha served Elijah and no mention is made of any great exploits of this great prophet.

We see Elisha cry out, "My father, my father..." and immediately following, his own life and ministry took shape.

Our churches became organized in the form of business models where we teach everything but the Principles of God, namely the unity of the home.

We'll teach doctrine and we'll preach anything that makes the people feel good. We'll talk about tithes and offerings, but the widows and orphans remain uncared for by and large. We love to

---

10 Rom. 8:16
11 Heb. 5:5

preach end time events and have people's expectations built up by these wonderful thoughts about the return of Christ, but that's where it remains.

Our churches are well decorated and furnished with the best, but at closer scrutiny, they are mostly foster homes that cater for orphans. They are not "homes" where hurting people can be changed into becoming sons and daughters.

Our world is in such disarray, with more problems than politics are able to fix. Scientists, Counselors, Doctors, Politicians, Lawmakers and the like, are unable to successfully address the issue of delinquent, confused and hurting people.

Thank God, more and more pastors are receiving this important revelation of how important it is to address this issue. However, too many are still looking *over the top* instead of *into* it.

When you study the Bible, you become acutely aware of the blueprint which the Father gave us. In fact, it is right in front of us to follow, but we don't. We build churches, not *homes*.

We build little "kingdoms" and forget to follow His plan.

Introducing Himself to mankind, God did this in the form of a "family." (See Figure 1)

He showed us how important the foundation must be. The home is not complete without a father and a mother in it!

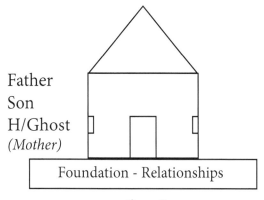

Figure 2

The foundation for the home is strong relationships in the family.

The Bible speaks about the Godhead, "Hear, Oh Israel: The Lord our God, is One Lord:"

This is the main reason families fall apart. The first thing that happens when a family breaks up is a corrupted relationship.

Families hardly communicate any longer. The dinner table has gone out the back-door. TV dinners are served while families spend valuable time in front of the box. Many homes have TV's in different rooms, so that each can watch their own programs. Kids have hardly any communication with parents any longer. The Bible is no longer read like families used to do it in times past. Prayer is no longer offered and God is only a religious fact in the minds of many and even that thought is waning fast.

The result is devastating to our Christian values and it is not strange to see the ever increasing rate of divorce climb through the ceiling.

According to Enrichment Journal on the divorce rate in America:

- The divorce rate in America for first marriage is 41%
- The divorce rate in America for second marriage is 60%
- The divorce rate in America for third marriage is 73%

Figure 3

39

You are reading this book because you are concerned, but it does not have to stop here. Before the "tumbling bricks" can be repaired in your home, go to the foundation. Get that right and *then* work on the walls!

4 ARE YOU A SON?

I was born into a family of fourteen children. We didn't think it was that much of an issue, since my uncle on dad's side, had over twenty children. (I don't know exactly how many, since I lost count at some stage.)

Mom and dad worked very hard to keep food on the table and they did an excellent job with that. I can never remember a day that we did not have enough food on the table. For us children, it was a given that there would be food.

There was very little time for play and as soon as you had any sense, dad expected you to bring your part.

At the age of twelve, I was fulltime employed after school, working in my dad's textile factory, and so were the other kids, **who were** older than **I.**

After work in the factory, I'd ride my bicycle ten miles to get home and then, after doing my chores around the house, homework came after supper.

There was not much time for playing during the week through Saturday's.

But we were a happy family. Mom had a great sense of humor, and dad was a good man.

He was very serious about life and I don't remember him ever playing with the kids. He was all work, and like many others of his time, came through the great depression and WWII.

The flaw in my memory about dad was the fact that he enjoyed his brandy. Dad changed when he drank and it did not take much for his raging temper to flare up after the first few drinks.

Therefore, all the children made it their business to stay out of his way, at least until he would summon anyone of us for a reason.

Looking back even today, I remember the passion in my heart as a young boy, to impress him. I loved my dad, but there were just too many things and too many other children around, for me to make any inroads into his busy agenda.

I was one of the middle children, and looking back today, I know my dad loved all of us dearly. He just did not know how to show it. A rub on the hair after a job well done, or a wink from his eye was about as much affection any of us would get. For some reason, my older brother got even less than that.

My dad took great pleasure in watching my brother and **me** fight. He was four years older than I, and if we did not fight each other, he enjoyed getting us into street fights. At a very young age, we were both introduced into the world of boxing.

As time went by, the distance between dad and **me** became wider, though I still carried with me the fantasy of pleasing him.

The situation with his drinking grew **worse** as time went by and many nights, Mom and some of us kids would overnight in a strangers house, as we fled from his raging temper.

Each time this happened, the separation between us would grow even wider.

I discovered Jesus as my Lord and Savior at the tender age of twelve, and though the problems with my father have been more than disturbing to me, I always regarded myself as a good son. I tried very hard and the development of my spirit by the Hand of God, directed me to remember his laws regarding honor to your parents.

Many years later and long after my father passed away, God started speaking to me about the subject of sonship.

When God spoke to me then, I'd already been in the ministry for more than twenty years and was raising a son and a daughter of our own, plus one adopted child.

I was anxious to start teaching people on the subject of true sonship, or as Jack Frost puts it, *"the embrace of the Father."*

God spoke to me, and said, "Yan, remember, before anyone can be a good father, they have to first be a good son."

I knew that I would pass that test as I always regarded myself as a good son. I've always tried to please my father. In fact, most of the children will agree, that if my dad had any favorite, they would pick me. He never did show favoritism to anyone and though I would not agree with them, I knew I lived a good life in front of my parents.

Nevertheless, I still asked God, "What do You say Lord? Am I *a son?"*

I fully expected God to hail my excellence. I expected nothing else, but to my amazement, God spoke clearly to me, and said, "No, you are not!"

I staggered, and for a moment I was confused, but then at the same moment, God brought an incident to my mind which I had totally forgotten about.

Resentment against my dad's drinking mistakes had built up a stronger resentment in me than I realized.

At the age of nineteen, my dad expected me to put a beating on someone he did not like, but the only problem was, I liked the man.

For the first time in my life, I went against my dad's wishes and told him I was not interested in picking a fight with this individual.

My dad conspired his own plan by putting all sorts of evil thoughts into this poor man's mind. Filling him with lies to the point where he became openly hostile to me. My dad promoted his courage so that when I got home from work one day, the boy was totally ready to fight me.

Standing behind him, my dad said, "He's too yellow to fight you, son."

For a while longer I tried to calm my friend, but my dad would have it no other way. "If he's not yellow, challenge him for a fight in the backyard."

I was totally stunned by my dad's actions, but still tried to remain calm. This boy, quite a bit taller, walked up to me, putting his face against mine, saying, "If you're not yellow, come fight me in the back then."

My mother came in between us, begging for this to stop. My heart was pounding inside my chest, for I did not want to hurt this friend of mine. However, he was beyond any consideration because of the many lies my dad put into his mind.

I knew what my dad wanted and it was so evil in my eyes. But, once again my dad stepped in, suggesting we go to a hill behind our home to fight. He left with my dad and when I started my car, my younger sister opened the passenger door, and as she sat down, looked at me, saying, "Yan, I cannot believe what dad has just done." I knew she was as confused.

Even as I write these lines, the memory of that pain tries to come back into my mind.

Getting out of the vehicle, still in a crouched position, my dad told Pete, "Don't try and box him because then you'll lose. When he get's out of the car, tackle him and take him down to the ground quick.

43

The boy did as he was told, but I connected him with a quick left hook that threw him back. For a second time, he rushed me like an amateur fighter, and I connected him for the second time, but not before his momentum pushed me back and I tripped over a rock behind me, falling to the ground.

My dad encouraged him to jump on top of me and as he did, I heard my dad say, "Take a rock and beat his head in!"

Suddenly I saw red. Throwing this big boy off of me like a sack of beans, I hit him with two or three hard blows to the face, and he surrendered with a bleeding nose.

I remembered that day when I slowly walked up to my dad, looking at him with anger I have never experienced before, saying, "You are not a father! I reject you as my father and will have nothing to do with you…"

Though we made peace in time to come, and I even helped him come back to Jesus years later, the break between father and son, became certain!

I still called him "dad" but something was broken. There was no longer a bond. One disappointment after another caused a definite break in our relationship.

All of this was hidden in yesterday's mist, as I asked God, "Am I a son?" and God said, "No."

At that moment it all came back to me and I left the presence of God, unfulfilled. I knew at that moment I could not preach this message until this matter became resolved.

But my father was no longer alive. He had long been buried and I remember my travail at his funeral. At that moment in God's presence, I realized how raw the wound still was and without me realizing it, I had walked away from my father on that hill with an "Orphaned Heart."

A short while later, I flew back to South Africa, visiting my dad's grave. I cried that day until I had no more tears to cry, like David once said.

I never realized how much rejection, pain and confusion had been buried in my heart until the day I opened my heart to the "atmosphere" around his grave.

I don't know if my dad could have heard my confession. I did not bring any accusation against him. I did not mention any of the emotional pain I experienced as a child. No, all I said was, "Dad, please forgive ME!"

Never before did I feel so "empty" as that day when I walked away from his grave. I cannot explain it, but it felt as if a huge void now appeared in my bosom.

Realizing what I was dealing with, namely an Orphaned Heart, I attended church that Sunday where the pastor did not know me. I went forward for prayer and allowed them to lay hands on me. However, I left even more "empty." I felt so unfulfilled.

On my way back to the USA, God spoke to me during the flight, saying to me, that an "Orphaned Spirit" cannot be cast out. It cannot be prayed out. It cannot be resolved with counsel. God said, the only way it can be resolved is by introducing the orphan to a "father."

I said, "But Lord, YOU are my Father!" God reminded me again of Paul's teaching when he told the Corinthian church, that "the natural comes first, THEN the spiritual."

Back in the USA, an old friend of mine connected with me shortly after, and that day, I heard God say, "Son, behold your father…"

JD became a father to me. I surrendered to his input into my life and suddenly my life changed as I became a son!

Shortly thereafter, I told God I'm ready to teach this message. Then God asked me, "Are you a father?"

I paused for a moment, then asked the Lord, "I don't know, what do You say, Lord?" For a moment there was silence, then I felt God say to me, "that's something you should ask your son…"

5 ARE YOU AFATHER?

When you hear the word, "father," what images come to mind? What about the word, "daddy?" Depending on what type of father you had growing up, these words can elicit very positive or very negative memories. Some children grow up with fathers who are actively and positively involved

> "My father didn't tell me how to live; he lived, and let me watch him do it."
> Clarence Kelland:

in their lives. These fathers love their children, spend time with them, praise them, play with them, protect them, teach them, and help them deal with the struggles of life. On the other hand, some children grow up with fathers who are very uninvolved or even fathers who left their responsibilities and moved elsewhere. Their actions do not convey love. They spend minimal amounts of time with their children; they do not encourage them, and they provide very little guidance.

What is the essence of fatherhood? Is it simply the establishment of biological paternity? Do fathers simply provide a paycheck? Or, does fatherhood encompass much more? Perhaps the more pertinent question is this: What constitutes responsible fatherhood? Responsible fatherhood cannot be proven with a blood test, nor does it consist of simply providing a paycheck. Responsible fatherhood cannot be reduced to a single dimension. It involves commitment, self-sacrifice, integrity, and unconditional love. Responsible fathers are concerned with the well-being of their children, and their desire is to see their children succeed in all areas of life.

While there are exceptions, the general rule is that children who have positively involved fathers tend to do better socially, emotionally, and academically than children whose fathers are not positively involved.

More and more, I find fathers absent in church while mothers and children attend. This is a clear indication of the intensity of this Orphan Epidemic that is tearing our nation apart.

William Shakespeare once wrote, "It is a wise father that knows his own child."

Broken Branches

In the United States alone, 21.2 million children (26% of all children) are growing up in a household with only one custodial parent.12

Among Black children, 48.5% are growing up with a single custodial parent.13

5 out of every 6 custodial parents are mothers (84%), 1 in 6 are fathers (16%).14

Poverty

Children in father-absent homes are five times more likely to be poor. In 2002, 7.8% of children in married-couple families were living in poverty, compared to 38.4% of children in female-householder families.15

Drug and Alcohol Abuse

The U.S. Department of Health and Human Services states, "Fatherless children are at a dramatically greater risk of drug and alcohol abuse."16 THESE FOOTNOTE NUMBERS SEEM TOO LARGE

Sexual Activity and Teen Pregnancy

Adolescent females between the ages of 15 and 19 years reared in homes without fathers are significantly more likely to engage in premarital sex than adolescent females reared in homes with both a

---

12 U.S. Census Bureau, Custodial Mothers and Fathers and Their Child Support: 2005, P60-234, August 2007
13 U.S. Census Bureau, Custodial Mothers and Fathers and Their Child Support: 2005, P60-234, August 2007
14 U.S. Census Bureau, Custodial Mothers and Fathers and Their Child Support: 2005, P60-234, August 2007
15 Source: U.S. Census Bureau, Children's Living Arrangements and Characteristics: March 2002, P20-547, Table C8. Washington, D.C.: GPO 2003
16 U.S. Department of Health and Human Services. National Center for Health Statistics. Survey on Child Health. Washington, DC, 1993.

mother and a father.17

Children in single parent families are more likely to get pregnant as teenagers than their peers who grow up with two parents.

Educational Achievement

In studies involving over 25,000 children using nationally representative data sets, children who lived with only one parent had lower grade point averages, lower college aspirations, poor attendance records, and higher drop out rates than students who lived with both parents.18

Fatherless children are twice as likely to drop out of school.

Crime

Children in single parent families are more likely to be in trouble with the law than their peers who grow up with two parents.19

The following question was posed to some of my readers: *"What is worst, a Physical Absent Father, or an Emotionally Absent Father."*

Note a few of the responses:

"Elsie" wrote: "I grew up with an emotionally absent father while my husband grew up with a physically absent father. We are both screwed up in our own individual ways. I think I came out on the better end, mainly because my parents were educated and my mom was very involved in our lives. My husband on the other hand, grew up with a mother who barely graduated high school and a physically abusive step father who couldn't read and write. Because the step father disliked him and his sister, the mother tended to side with her husband. Essentially he grew up with a physically absent father, an emotionally distant mother and emotionally distant step father.

---

17 Billy, John O. G., Karin L. Brewster and William R. Grady. "Contextual Effects on the Sexual Behavior of Adolescent Women." Journal of Marriage and Family 56 (1994)

18 McLanahan, Sara and Gary Sandefur. Growing up with a Single Parent: What Hurts, What Helps. Cambridge: Harvard University Press, 1994.

19 U.S. Department of Health and Human Services. National Center for Health Statistics. National Health Interview Survey. Hyattsville, MD, 1988.

"Matt" wrote: "As much as a father is important in a child's life, if he isn't going to show any affection/time to him/her, then that child is going to grow up thinking that is how men are supposed to be.

A male child may become emotionally distant because I said to myself, "If that's the way he is, then I guess that's what I should be like. The results were disastrous."

"Julie" wrote: "Children come to mainly love and feel secure by those who are around them on a daily basis. In many homes, a mother is the only parent available for the child. With all due respect, in some homes it is the father who is the main caregiver.

Overall, as it concerns the children however, a parent who is physically absent provides fewer negatives in the child's life than a parent who is around a lot but obviously doesn't care about the child.

That's like being hurt emotionally over and over because they "see" the parent doesn't really care about them. Kids are so much smarter than we give them credit for.

Oh, my life could have been so different if I just knew that I was loved. I hate what has become of me."

"Jean' wrote: "Does it really matter? They are both not fulfilling the role of a father and are both hard to deal with. However, I think it would be more painful to see your father at home and him not pay any attention to you vs. the father that just never comes around because you don't see him and don't think about it as much.

In any case, why "father" someone if you're not going to care for them? That's why this world including me, are in such a mess!"

After many years of teaching the body of Christ and at the point where I was ready to present this teaching to the church, I needed to find out what my status as a father was. God told me to go and ask my son, so I made the appointment to see him.

I made double sure that there would be no interruptions during our conversation and he had no idea what I wanted to talk about.

CJ, my oldest son, one of the dearest people I know, has always looked up to me. In fact, I was sure that he admired me and yet, for the previous years, I noticed a "drifting apart" between us.

There were no problems that I knew of, but the close embrace just was not there between us any longer, and it troubled me greatly.

"So dad, what is it you want to talk about?" He asked it with a smile, but I could see that he was anxious to find out what the meeting was all about.

My emotions were running full and when I spoke, I had to fight to keep it from showing in my voice. CJ noticed, but decided to just remain quiet.

"I want to ask you CJ, please tell me what you think of me as a father." That was about as much I could get out without cracking up in front of him.

"Dad, what are you talking about? You're a fantastic father! You're my hero, and I love you."

I smiled and remained quiet for a few moments but then encouraged him to "come clean." I explained to him what was going on and how the Lord encouraged me to ask him the question about my status as a father.

I got up from the chair I was sitting in and placed myself on the floor in front of him.

"Please son, today I need you to open your heart to me like never before. I promise you I will not defend myself. I will only listen to you."

Suddenly the flood gate of his emotions opened and it started pouring out of him. He took me back to moments I had forgotten about. He reminded me of how much it hurt when I missed a special ball game of his and how my wife and I left him alone at home to go and visit church people. He went on and on and both of us cried as he poured his heart out.

I've been in full-time ministry since he was a little boy and now, deep into his thirties, he invited me into his lonely world.

I sat there, sobbing my heart out. I never knew about how much this mattered to him. I didn't realize what those things did to his emotions, but I realized he was offering me a rare opportunity by opening the door to his heart, and I wanted back in with all my might!

When he was all done, I humbly knelt in front of him, and with both our faces freshly washed with tears, I lifted up my one finger and asked him, "Do you think you can give me ONE-MORE chance at this? I really love you son, and I would love to be a father to you…"

As we embraced that day, for the first time in years I discovered realness in our friendship.

Several years have passed since that day, but I can proudly say, "He's my son and I am his father."

Dad, as you read this book, ask yourself, or even better still, find out for yourself, if you ARE a father!

After years of professional pondering, one day this hit me. When you strip everything away from our lives and focus in on our most basic, fundamental need, what's most important? When you strip everything away and drill down to the center of our soul, what do we crave the most? My answer…to be loved. I thought about what is the most important, most valuable, most critical "thing" that I need. After some thought, it came down to… love. I want to love others and I want to be loved. Love. That's it. Love!

Now, if I had a choice, who would I prefer to be loved by? I can show love to anyone. But who are the most important people for me to love? Answer: I want to love my family, and I want to be loved by them as well. It all goes back to our families.

So, the most important thing in the life of a child, is to hear words that communicates the father loves for him/her.

Could it be the reason why the father's blessing is so powerful? Because he's the most important person in the life of a child, fulfilling the most critical need in his/her life, by employing the most powerful force in universe, the spoken word?

When you build your family's future, you have to do it on the blueprint God set for us. Nothing else and nothing less. It has to be done using God, the Father, as a guiding post.

Healthy relationships in the home, around the dinner table, when you come and when you go, is the glue that keeps them together. When the storms do come, and they will, it will be the strong bond of unity that keep the circumstances of life outside the boat. Yes, when the storms come and when the winds blow, the house will remain standing because of the solid foundation. That foundation is real, lasting relationships built and established through loving outreach to one another.

The boat is designed to float, and no matter how fierce the storm, it will survive.

Jesus once said, "If a house is divided against itself, that house will not be able to stand."[20]

Later, the Lord also said, " "Therefore everyone who hears these words of mine and puts them into practice is like a wise man who built his house on the rock. [25] The rain came down, the streams rose, and the winds blew and beat against that house; yet it did not fall, because it had its foundation on the rock."[21]

DOING IT GOD'S WAY

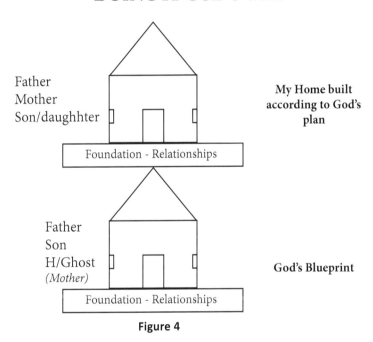

Father
Mother
Son/daughhter

My Home built
according to God's
plan

Foundation - Relationships

Father
Son
H/Ghost
(Mother)

God's Blueprint

Foundation - Relationships

Figure 4

Our nation is hurting from the bottom up. Children are oft turned into monsters, pursuing love and acceptance in all the wrong places.

They're killing each other and our leaders are trying to rectify the problem with legislation.

---

[20] Mark 3:25
[21] Mathew 7:24-25

We can try all we please, but the problem is:

We've taken God out of the homes, out of the streets, the schools, the courts and everywhere else.

It is the Lord who will uphold our values. Without him in our lives, we build the house in vain. Without following His blueprint, our homes are built and designed for destruction.

Secondly, we are trying to build our homes on "The American Dream," instead of on a strong foundation of good, healthy relationships.

We pursue the dollar, we pursue pleasure, we chase after everything that is vanity and the results are devastating.

Spiritual storms ravaged our country and broken branches are visibly noticed in all walks of life.

Decide with me today, to go back to the plan which God gave us right from the beginning and build your home according to His design.

It is not too late!

6 TEACHERS, BUT NO FATHERS

There is absolutely no doubt in my mind that our nation can be healed again, but the role of the church **has** to be drastically altered to conform to the plan of God.

The "Orphan Spirit" **has** prevailed since the beginning of time, and as I mentioned earlier in this book, **it is** the offspring of the "father of lies."

> **1 Cor. 4:15**
>
> **For though you may have ten thousand teachers in Christ, you do not have many fathers...**

Therefore, Jesus made it abundantly clear to his disciples, that He would not leave them as orphans, but would introduce them to His Father in heaven.

Not only does the church have to deal with the spiritual offspring of the enemy, but also the multitudes who have become "Broken Branches" as a result of a failing society!

The problem we are facing in an unbelievably wide spectrum, is that the church is failing miserably in its responsibilities.

People with orphan hearts, wounded on the journey of life, are floating from church to church, often unable to find satisfaction.

They are NOT looking for a better program, or a comfortable church with professional décor. They are looking for identity, protection, discipline and fatherly love.

Unfortunately though, in so many cases it is not found, because we've turned our churches into Foster-Homes! Too often, our beautiful buildings are nothing more than professional, commercialized institutions and the agendas of so many of these establishments offer everything but the 'household of God!" The church should be a "Father's House," where orphans are changed into becoming sons and daughters!

Instead, we try to "lure" them into our facilities, because the more "foster children" we can house, the better the financial benefits!

Inside these foster homes, people remain lonely, indifferent and unfulfilled.

We've scooped the cream off the top of the gospel and offer them healing, deliverance, a promise of the second coming of Christ and lame Sunday school lessons. We teach them our philosophies and doctrines, but at the end of each service, they return to broken and divided homes!

In fact, most churches and pastors remain oblivious to what goes on in these homes. They try to "fix" people's lives in the ineffective prayer lines of our church gatherings.

When these troubled people still receive "a touch from the Lord," they merely go back to the same crumbled lives to live in the confusion and mire they find themselves trapped in.

This problem has taken on epidemic proportions and is spreading by the hour!

We cannot build the church house on a false foundation! It also, must be built according to the blueprint of God!

Paul, corrected the Corinthian church, by saying, *"For though you have ten thousand teachers, you do not have many fathers!"*

Ask God to help you get this into your mind and soul! We cannot and must not try to develop a "new breed of elephants" without the strong influence of fathers. The results have always proven fatal and we're seeing it unfold in front of our eyes.

It does not work in nature, and neither will it work in a nation!

This is not the idea of a man, but it is the fundamental principal of all creation. When there is no father, there is no future!

Look at what Psalms 68:5-7 says about God: *"Sing to God, sing praises to His name; Lift up a song for Him who rides through the deserts, Whose name is the LORD, and exult before Him. A father of the fatherless and a judge for the widows, Is God in His holy habitation. God makes a home for the lonely.."*

Many of our churches are built as "little kingdoms", each separately functioning on their own. The influence of "fathers" on the "children" are almost non-existent. What we have most of the time are deacons and elders who don't even understand what their role should be in the HOUSE of God.

Please don't misunderstand me. I don't mean to be cynical or critical of the overall church. But we're not doing something right, are we? We're losing our youth and the general population in our society **has** lost faith in the integrity of the church.

We're preaching sermons and practicing fancy programs but at the same time, find ourselves sucked into the quagmire of confusion that is destroying our generation!

The church cannot be built separately as its own entity! It has to be built on the successful model which God put in front of us!

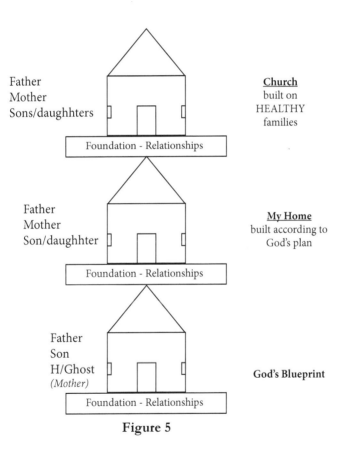

Father
Mother
Sons/daughhters

Church
built on
HEALTHY
families

Foundation - Relationships

Father
Mother
Son/daughhter

My Home
built according to
God's plan

Foundation - Relationships

Father
Son
H/Ghost
(Mother)

God's Blueprint

Foundation - Relationships

Figure 5

We just have to get this right if we want to turn this generation back to God!

In these troubled times, people are keeping their eyes on the "Eastern Sky", waiting for the return of our Savior. They try and tell the "times" and observe the "blood moons" but seem to overlook one of the great prophecies for our time.

Mal. 4:5-6, Behold, I will send you Elijah the prophet before the coming of the great and dreadful day of the Lord:

And he shall *turn the heart of the fathers to the children, and the heart of the children to their fathers*, lest I come and smite the earth with a curse.

What does Elijah represent?

Elijah was a great prophet but when one really **analyzes** his role at the time, then you notice how he turned an Elisha into a son!

The day when Elijah was taken up into heaven, the young disciple looked up and cried, "_My father! My father! The chariots and horsemen of Israel!_"[22]

Elijah's mission was completed after he turned a hard working boy into a son.

That same spirit is promised to come back to the end-time church. The "fathering spirit", which will call a halt to this epidemic that is threatening to destroy our society.

The church need a fresh injection of true, spiritual fathers who in turn, will make it their mission to turn the many orphans in our pews into real sons of God.

To be a _father_ will take more than mere gray hairs or a life long involvement in the church. To be a _father_, you need to develop a _son_.

A son does not leave his position at the side of a father. Several times, Elijah tested the young Elisha by saying, "Tarry here while I **go on.**" Take time to read the account again:[23]

And it came to pass, when the Lord would take up Elijah into heaven by a whirlwind, that Elijah went with Elisha from Gilgal.

2 And Elijah said unto Elisha, Tarry here, I pray thee; for the Lord hath sent me to Bethel. And Elisha said unto him, As the Lord liveth, and as thy soul liveth, I will not leave thee. So they went down to Bethel.

3 And the sons of the prophets that were at Bethel came forth to Elisha, and said unto him, Knowest thou that the Lord will take away thy master from thy head to day? And he said, Yea, I know it; hold ye your peace.

4 And Elijah said unto him, Elisha, tarry here, I pray thee; for the Lord hath sent me to Jericho. And he said, As the Lord liveth, and as thy soul liveth, I will not leave thee. So they came to Jericho.

---

[22] 2 Kings 2:12
[23] 2 Kings 2

5 And the sons of the prophets that were at Jericho came to Elisha, and said unto him, Knowest thou that the Lord will take away thy master from thy head to day? And he answered, Yea, I know it; hold ye your peace.

6 And Elijah said unto him, Tarry, I pray thee, here; for the Lord hath sent me to Jordan. And he said, As the Lord liveth, and as thy soul liveth, I will not leave thee. And they two went on.

7 And fifty men of the sons of the prophets went, and stood to view afar off: and they two stood by Jordan.

8 And Elijah took his mantle, and wrapped it together, and smote the waters, and they were divided hither and thither, so that they two went over on dry ground.

9 And it came to pass, when they were gone over, that Elijah said unto Elisha, Ask what I shall do for thee, before I be taken away from thee. And Elisha said, I pray thee, let a double portion of thy spirit be upon me.

10 And he said, Thou hast asked a hard thing: nevertheless, if thou see me when I am taken from thee, it shall be so unto thee; but if not, it shall not be so.

11 And it came to pass, as they still went on, and talked, that, behold, there appeared a chariot of fire, and horses of fire, and parted them both asunder; and Elijah went up by a whirlwind into heaven.

12 And Elisha saw it, and he cried, My father, my father, the chariot of Israel, and the horsemen thereof.

When I look at how easy it has become for people to switch churches in our times, then it tells me right away what is really going on. They are not sons!

I'm trying to get pastors to understand the importance of this matter, because when people walk through the doors of your church, the likelihood is great that they are prodigals and need the embrace of a father.

The difference between a child and a son.

Coming into the Kingdom of God, does not automatically qualify you to be a son or a daughter. That is an earned position.

In the book of John, we are told that, *"as many as received him, to them gave he power to become the sons of God, even to them that believe on his name."*

After accepting Christ in your life, you become born again into a new family. Paul says, *"The Spirit bears witness with our spirits that we are children of God."*[24]

The word "children" in the Greek means, "TEKNON." In the Strong's concordance, it is defined as [5043 Téknon – properly, a child]. It means such a person is fully dependent on another.

Consider such a person in the light of a toddler, or someone who have not yet matured and therefore can only be trusted with menial tasks.

When such a person walks away from a father, or the father walks away from him/her, they act and behave as an orphan, with zero sense of direction. They lose all sense of identity and don't feel like they belong anywhere. They cannot make it on their own and **are** susceptible to all sorts of adverse influences.

A "Téknon" also means "one who follows in the shoes of another." They are influenced by anyone who leaves their imprint in their lives. (Refer to Page 13 on "Imprinting.")

Until such a person is properly "imprinted" by the Father, they are in danger of becoming adversely affected by another "father."

When such a Téknon is influenced by the father of lies, who produces orphans, they will no longer act and behave as a child (Téknon) of God, but as an orphan."

The Orphan Spirit can not be "cast out of a person." Remember. the only way to help such a person is to introduce them to a "father."

In Rom. 8:14, Paul makes it clear when he explains, *"For as many as are led by the Spirit of God, they are the sons of God."*

The "as many" denotes *"those."* Or only those. It speaks of

---

24 Rom 8:16

ONLY those who allow themselves to be "*led*" by the Spirit. Not everyone or anyone. "*Those who are led,*" by the Spirit. Those who allow the "*Father of Lights,*" to imprint them so that they become like Him.

The word "led" can also be translated as "*controlled.*" When you get to the place where you finally say, "Not my will, but Thine be done."

OBEDIENCE is not an easy process. It does not happen overnight. It is a process that involves suffering. It is a process that demands the involvement of "tutors." It demands a slave-like obedience until God decides you are ready to accept son-ship!

Gal. 4:1-3 [Message bible] makes it clear. "*Let me show you the implications of this. As long as the heir is a minor, he has no advantage over the slave. Though legally he owns the entire inheritance, he is subject to tutors and administrators until whatever date the father has set for emancipation. That is the way it is with us: When we were minors, we were just like slaves ordered around by simple instructions (the tutors and administrators of this world), with no say in the conduct of our own lives.*"

Okay then, let's read the verse again in the light of my explanation: "Only those ones who allow themselves to be controlled by the impulses of the Spirit under the guidance of tutors (Or fathers) are recognized as sons of God."

Keep in mind, that the "Blueprint" of God, is applied throughout, and even though Christ Jesus was God as a person, Paul teaches in Heb. 5:8: "*Although He was a Son, He learned obedience from the things which He suffered*"

In fact, we don't read about any ministry on His part before He was baptized by John. What happened after the baptism that "kick-started" His ministry?

The voice of the Father spoke and testified for all to hear, even throughout the millenniums, when He said, "*This is my beloved Son, in whom I am well pleased.*" From that day on, His recorded ministry started.

Finally, in Heb. 5, Paul talks about the honor of being called by God for ministry. He explains carefully, that no one can take up that position without being approved by the Father. Let's take a closer **look:** "*And no man takes this honor unto himself, but he that is called of God, as was Aaron.*

So also Christ glorified not himself to be made an high priest; but he that said unto him, Thou art my Son, to day have I begotten thee."

Dr. Mark Hanby , in his book "You Have Not Many Fathers", asserts that the reason why the church as whole is not completely walking in the fullness of the power and influence that God desires is "because we have lost respect for the order of transferring power from one generation to the next; that order is <u>from fathers to sons</u>. Fathers (i.e. mentors or elders) are there to identify the potential within a person and assist them in developing and releasing it to the fullest. This relationship is affirming to a son or daughter (i.e. mentee/pupil), allowing him or her to be sent forth into his or her destiny wearing a coat of confidence and assurance of identity, purpose, and power. Sadly, one of the greatest attacks we face as a generation is the total destruction and/or perversion of this most holy and most necessary order. Without it, this generation has been lost and stranded in a wilderness, possessing greatness on the inside that never reaches its fullness. If we are to rescue our generation and the purpose of God that lives within our hearts, we have to restore God's order by reconciling the hearts of spiritual fathers to the hearts of their sons."

7 DESTINY ON HOLD

There are many stories in the bible which the church presents wrong and the story of Jacob is one of them.

After 20 years of marriage, Isaac prayed for a child and God answered the call. Rebekah became pregnant. She felt the babies moving inside her (apparently a little more movement than she had expected), so she asked God why this was happening. God replied, telling Rebekah that "two nations" were in her womb, she was pregnant with twins, and a battle was already being waged inside her.

God told Rebekah that one of the twins would be stronger than the other and that, opposite of what tradition would normally dictate, the younger one would rule over the firstborn.

In the days of old, names were given to children with prophetic intent.

When asked what the name of Jacob means, the answer is always given in the wrong, namely, his name means "deceiver."

While that is true, his name however, actually carried a double meaning, namely "Supplanter/Contender", and "Deceiver."

It is absolutely absurd to even imagine that any loving mother, would name her child "deceiver." Especially since God told Rebekah that Jacob was going to be the spiritual leader of His people.

The reality of God's foreknowledge manifested when the truth played out with Esau, the older brother, dishonoring his birthright and cheapened it by accepting a pot of stew in the place of that favor.[25]

Esau revealed his true character by saying "Behold, I am going to die: and what profit shall this birthright do to me?" These words show what a low estimate he placed upon "the blessing of Abraham."

This birthright he *contemptuously* termed it. We think, too, that in the light of the surrounding circumstances Esau's utterance here

---

[25] Gen. 25:27-34

explains the word of the Holy Spirit in Hebrews 12:16—"*Lest there be any fornicator, or profane person, as Esau, who for one morsel of meat sold his birthright.*"

Surely Esau did not mean he would die of hunger unless he ate immediately of the pottage, for that is scarcely conceivable when he had access to all the provisions in Isaac's house.

And it came to pass, that when Isaac was old, and his eyes were dim, so that he could not see, he called Esau his eldest son, and said unto him, "My son: and he said unto him, Behold, here am I. Behold now, I am old, I know not the day of my death: Now therefore take, I pray thee, thy weapons, thy quiver and thy bow, and go out to the field, and take me some venison; And make me savory meat, such as I love, and bring it to me, that I may eat; that my soul may bless thee before I die" (Gen. 27:1-4).

Why was it that Isaac desired to partake of venison from Esau before blessing him? Does not Genesis 25:28 answer the question—"And Isaac loved Esau because he did eat of his venison."

In view of this statement it would seem, then, that Isaac desired to enkindle or intensify his affections for Esau, so that he might bless him with all his heart. But surely Isaac's eyes were "dim" spiritually as well as physically.

Let us not forget that what we read here at the beginning of Genesis 27 follows immediately after the record of Esau marrying the two heathen wives. Thus it will be seen that Isaac's wrong in being partial to Esau was greatly aggravated by treating so lightly his son's affront to the glory of Jehovah...and all for a meal of venison! Alas, what a terrible thing is the flesh with its "affections and lusts" even in a believer, yea, more terrible than in an unbeliever.

But worst of all, Isaac's partiality toward Esau was a plain disregard of God's word to Rebekah that Esau should "serve" Jacob (Gen. 25:23).

Since Rebekah knew about the "sold out" of Esau's birthright, it is purely inconceivable that Isaac did not know about it as well.

Our camera has the ability to zoom in for a close-up shot to focus and isolate a very small area. It also has the ability to zoom out to get what is known as a wide-angle shot. This is also called the panoramic view. It gives the broader picture.

Zooming out, we see Isaac and Esau huddled together in an

intensely animated conversation. Their heads bob and weave. Fingers puncture the air as their hands rise, fall, twist, and turn.

Suddenly, Esau leaves the house with quiver and arrows in hand. He disappears over a distant knoll apparently on another hunting trip. His fast pace and long strides tell us he is in an unusual hurry.

What Isaac and Esau do not see, but we can, is Rebekah standing just around the corner listening to the entire conversation. She has long suspected something was afoot between these two but at last it is confirmed. She listens as Isaac says to Esau, "Take your quiver and your bow, and go out to the field and hunt game for me. And make me savory food, such as I love, and bring it to me that I may eat, that my soul may bless you before I die."

Although she had long suspected it she can't believe it is about to happen. Isaac is about to pull off an end-around maneuver against the revealed will of God.

He knows God's will in this matter--"The elder shall serve the younger"--but he seems determined to totally disregard it by favoring Esau above Jacob. I

Isaac says he wants it to happen "before I die." What do you mean, Isaac, "before I die!?" You will live for another 40-years!

Isaac is determined to pull off a scheme that will favor his favorite son. His sensual appetites totally dominate him even as Esau's did, allowing Jacob to wrest the birthright from him. Like father, like son.

Now it will be Rebekah's turn to put into high gear her own scheme that has the same purpose to favor her favorite son. We are about to witness the other side of the coin: like mother, like son.

This is indeed a family split right down the middle. It will prove to be a valuable lesson based upon the theory that, "the end justifies the means." Rebekah will try to solve God's problem of getting Jacob to the head of the class before Isaac botches the whole process.

When Isaac discovered that he had blessed Jacob instead of Esau he "trembled very exceedingly."

This was the turning point in the incident, the point where, for the first time, light breaks in on this dark scene. It was horror which was awakened in his soul as he now fully realized that he had been pitting himself against the expressed mind of Jehovah.

It is beautiful to notice that instead of "cursing" Jacob (as his son had feared), now that Isaac discovers how God had graciously overruled his wrong doing, he bowed in self-judgment, and "trembled with a great trembling."

Then it was that faith found expression in the words "*And he shall be blest*" (v. 33).

He knew now that God had been securing what He had declared before the sons were born. It is this which the Spirit seizes on in Hebrews 11:20, "*By faith Isaac blest Jacob and Esau concerning things to come.*"

Go Home, Jacob

One of the saddest stories in the bible is what happened to Jacob for the following twenty years.

He departed from his father's presence and fled to a far away place, falling into the hands of his deceiving uncle, Laban.

He ran away saying "*I have deceived my father*," and for the years to follow, adopted the second meaning of his name, namely "deceiver."

What a terrible thing to live with such condemnation over your life?

The question should be asked though, "Did he really deceive his father, since the birthright was his by a contract of sale?"

Sure, the way he and his mother went about doing it was deceitful, but at the same time they were dealing with a father who blinded himself to the wrongs of a son who showed no regard for the integrity of the birthright.

Then, we witness the ensuing years of living far beneath the level of God's destiny for his life, with constant fear of what the future will hold for him.

Looking back at the life of this "father of the faith," we can clearly see how he became a "broken branch." Severed from the generational destiny which God intended for him.

Nothing would work out for him until he would heed the advice from God to "Go Home!"

In fact, on his flight to Egypt as he ran away from home, God appeared to him in a dream and reaffirmed His promise to him[26] about his destiny.

And Jacob rose up early in the morning, and took the stone that he had put for his pillows, and set it up for a pillar, and poured oil upon the top of it.

And he called the name of that place Bethel: but the name of that city was called Luz at the first.

And Jacob vowed a vow, saying, If God will be with me, and will keep me in this way that I go, and will give me bread to eat, and raiment to put on, so that I come again to my father's house in peace; then shall the Lord be my God:

---

[26] Gen 28: 11-21

Yet, he continued on his prodigal journey which would put destiny on halt for twenty years!

It is truly amazing how man can continue on his folly in spite of the caution of God.

In Gen 31, God meets with Jacob again, saying, "I am the God of Bethel, where you anointed the pillar, and where you vowed a vow unto me: now arise, get thee out from this land, and <u>return unto the land of thy father</u>."

"Nothing can really happen for you Jacob, unless you go home", is the message given to him from God.

On his way home, an angel meets with him again, wrestling with him through the night, and finally asks the one important question that would forever change his destiny, *"What is your name?"*

Like so many times in the past, he answers by saying, "My name is Jacob – 'deceiver.'"

The angel then does something remarkable, by saying to him, "Thy name shall be called no more Jacob, but Israel: for as a prince hast thou power with God and with men, and hast prevailed."

For Jacob to accept his destiny and finally "go home," he had to get his mind straight.

He had to change the way he thought about himself. He had to go home as an overcomer, a prince who has power with God!

He had to go home, as a true son to his father and shake loose the pain of the past.

Dear reader, why not ask God to help **you** close the door on yesterday. Put all the failures and hurt behind you. Accept the responsibilities of a true son/daughter in the natural, despite the pains and disappointments which caused you to be ruptured from the umbilical cord of your destiny.

"Go Home Jacob!" This is the message to our nation. Get your house in order, get the church back on track by fully concentrating on the full purpose of God for our lives, namely to build a home with a complete family inside, namely a father, mother and children, bound by the strong bond of close relationships.

Pastor, make up your mind today, to turn your church into a house of fathers and sons…

ABOUT THE AUTHOR

I have been married to Yan for 46 wonderful, blessed years. He has always been a true "Father" to our home. Our kids were taught to not only respect him but also to honor him as the head of our home.

During these 46 years, he showed himself as a true husband and a good father to our children. Someone who can be called "daddy" in the true sense of the word.

I can honestly say that he never faltered in his call as the head of our home.

Not only has he proven himself as a father to our children, but in the household of God, he has proven himself as a father of the faith.

I love you Honey, and may the people reading this book find the true meaning of the word "Father."

Elizabeth Venter

35220488R00042

Made in the USA
Charleston, SC
02 November 2014